PRINCESS SHARDE
KINGDOM OF THEE

This fairytale takes place in the Kingdom of Thee. Princess Sharde, through whimsical and enchanting interactions with its inhabitants, is magically transformed into the kingdom itself, for little girls and fairytales it's all in the kingdom of Thee. Unicorn's Mermaid's Crown's and Court Juster's in the Kingdom Of Thee. Butterflies and Doves with beautiful rainbow eagles eyes fly and adorn the blue skyline above the Kingdom of Thee. Princess Sharde comes out on her balcony and plays along with all of great magically tales of Thee. Looking at the beautiful mermaids swinging by the sea humbly at dawn singing the wonderful whimsical songs that echoes the Kingdom of Thee. What Princess Sharde truly longs for is true friendships to adorn her in the magical realm of Thee.

I am Sharde, the Princess of the Kingdom of Thee.

I have everything brought to me, you see. Being a Princess is so rewarding to me.

My whimsical friends never pertain to value me because we are all apart of the kingdom of Thee.

I have many friends who flown at me and say they love me that live in the rim of thee but do they love me because I am their princess.

How can that be? They do not come over and play with me.

True friendship are made with people who accept you for being kind, and not just for being whimsical.

Thinking life treats me
like all things are mine.

I am thought of being very refined, treated like a pearl in rainbow, living inside a white marble clam shell.

That image and representation doesn't reflect the real me.

I am viewed this way because I am Princess Sharde the Princess of Thee.

To have a friendship between you and me, I will be The Princess Sharde the way I was meant to be. The girl that lives in your town, in the Kingdom of Thee.

I just want to have good friends in the kingdom you see who, will appreciate me for me.

Know that I am not just the Princess of Thee, I am more than what you thought I could be.

I don't need anyone else to validate me.

Being The Princess of Thee is like Shangri-La to me.

Made in the USA
Columbia, SC
30 November 2024

48014894R00020